Victorian Style

Victorian Style

Classic Homes of North America

by Cheri Y. Gay

COURAGE BOOKS

AN IMPRINT OF
RUNNING PRESS BOOK PUBLISHERS

Philadelphia • London

Library of Congress Cataloging-in-Publication Number 2001094666

ISBN 0-7624-1312-3

First published in 2002 by
PRC Publishing Ltd,
64 Brewery Road, London N7 9NT
A member of the Chrysalis Group plc

Published by Courage Books, an imprint of
Running Press Book Publishers
125 South Twenty-second Street
Philadelphia, PA 19103-4399

This book may be ordered by mail from the publisher. **But try your bookstore first!**

Visit us on the web!
www.runningpress.com

Acknowledgements

I am grateful to the Detroit Public Library for its breadth and depth of resources that
provided the research materials for this book, and to the entire staff of the library's Art & Literature
department who were particularly helpful and patient with my numerous requests.
Also, a special thank you to my brother Ron Gay for reading the manuscript and making
insightful suggestions. And to my husband, Giancarlo Castillo, thank you for
your numerous readings of the text, and most of all for your forbearance.

Contents

Introduction

One hundred years ago the Victorian period officially ended along with the reign of England's Queen Victoria. It was an era of ornate eclecticism sandwiched between periods of simplicity. Preceding the Victorian era, the clean lines of classical and early American architecture styles predominated in North America. By the end of the century, a cacophony of architectural and interior designs had overlapped, coexisted, and competed with one another, to culminate in, almost with a sigh of relief, the plain forms of the Arts and Crafts Movement.

What today is termed Victorian is really a series of architectural styles, most of them imitative of earlier periods from Europe and Great Britain. Though the United States was seeking its identity, culturally, politically, socially, and artistically, it sustained strong ties to its European heritage. In 1872, American painter William Merritt Chase was heard to remark, on being asked if he would like to go abroad, "My God, I'd rather go to Europe than go to heaven."

The ambivalence between striking out as a young nation with ideas of its own and the desire to emulate the sophistication of England and the Continent was exemplified in the mixture and blend of architectural and interior styles during the Victorian period.

An endless number of books have been published on all aspects of the Victorian age, not the least on its architecture and interior designs. While the Victorians renewed and reinvented architectural styles of the past which they felt reflected the highest in moral and artistic merit, the Victorian period in turn continues to be imitated and recreated today.

The era was a time of great technological advances and rapid social change, corresponding perhaps to a similar period in our own time. Like the Victorians, we are a nation of nesters, tirelessly decorating, repairing, and improving our homes, to create havens from the strain and bustle of the outside world. A number of restored Victorian homes exist around the country and are seen as cozy retreats from the harsh clamor of daily life. Indeed, a culture of bed and breakfast establishments in Victorian homes appeals to the escapism in us.

In the following pages, take a pictorial stroll through some of the glorious homes from that era to learn about the architecture, furniture, and design that fascinate us still. Trace the beginnings of the Victorian era, from its classical period of Greek and Italian revival, to the Renaissance and Gothic revivals emphasizing Christian symbolism. Follow the changing styles—the French Second Empire phase, with its contribution of the mansard roof, followed by the inventiveness of the Queen Anne era, to the end of the century and the reactionary forces of the Stick and Shingle styles and the Arts and Crafts Movement.

Left: This cozy-looking children's playroom in Hayward, California shows the kind of entertainments that were available to youngsters at this time. There are different types of dolls, a rocking horse, and the table is set for an anticipated tea party.

The kaleidoscope of home designs paralleled changes effected by the Industrial Revolution: mass production; railroad, telegraph, and telephone connecting East Coast to West; the development of water and sewer systems, and the progression of lighting from kerosene to gas to electricity. All of these changes, and their resulting social ramifications, were reflected in the ways the Victorians lived.

By the end of the century, an agrarian society had moved into the cities and created new communities called suburbs. People began vigorously consuming the natural resources around them and outputting new, consumer goods. Family-oriented households turned outward to involvement in social movements and to work outside the home, for money to buy consumer goods. When the Victorian era ended, electric light had turned night into day, forever disrupting nature's rhythms.

Some have divided the era of 1837–1901 into a Romantic and a Victorian period, separated by the Civil War, calling Victorian only those houses with flamboyant styles made possible by balloon framing and technology that eliminated the need for the handcraftsmanship of timber frame building. However, most writers and scholars of that era merely ascribe a romantic aspect to the beginning of the period, adding the moniker "The Gilded Age," coined by Mark Twain, to aptly describe the heyday of the Victorians, 1870 through the end of the century.

Not a history book, not a book of interior design how-tos, this visual tour takes a look at the nature of the Victorian home inside and out, with descriptions and explanations of architectural features and typical rooms, illustrated by color photographs of houses around the country.

Left, above: This mid-century dining room in Cape May, New Jersey, displays all the High Victorian features of Turkish-influenced window dressing, tri-partite walls, a Rococo Revival sideboard with its showy display of silver, and a fanciful table centerpiece.

Left, below: This is the Cupples House, in St. Louis, Missouri, and is one of the best examples of Richardsonian Romanesque architecture of the period, with its turrets, stonework, and arched entranceway.

Right: Furnished in the style of 1860s, the Rains House in California demonstrates a simple approach to entry décor. Though not as sizeable as some entryways, it still has the welcoming components of chairs and a table.

Exterior Architecture

When the words "Victorian house" are uttered, an image instantly springs to mind, though in truth, there is no architectural category by the name "Victorian." The fanciful gingerbread clapboard dwelling, with its dizzying array of towers, gables, spindles, and porches is but one of many architectural genres, or combination of genres, that existed during that era.

Since the Victorian period began in 1837 and lasted until 1901, it is impossible that any one style of architecture could have dominated for that long. What *was* a predominant feature of that era was how classical British and European architectural models were adapted to suit North American tastes, raw materials, and technology.

The advent of new technologies such as the balloon framed house, where standard-sized pieces of machine-cut lumber, uniformly spaced, and held together by machine-made nails, replaced the hand-hewn post and beam structures of the past, meant that more people could own homes. House plans by mail, at the end of the 1840s, when readers of *Godey's Lady's Book* could order any one of 450 house styles, followed by mail order catalogs of houses themselves, after the Civil War, also played a part in the evolution and proliferation of house styles.

Architectural genres at the beginning of the Victorian period reflected the moral rectitude and values of the population. Family life was paramount and people were close to and involved with their communities, exemplified if you will by the square and sturdy timber framed building techniques. By the time balloon framed building construction was in full swing, the creatively shaped rooms and appendages of houses fully represented the expanding and diversified nature of American life, at home and nationally.

Though a symbol of the earliest democracy, Greek architecture was considered a "modern architecture" in North America. Sparked by interest in architectural discoveries in Greece and Rome, and, after the War of 1812, by a growing disenchantment with things British, Greek Revival was the first architectural model of the Victorian period, although it began some years earlier, around 1820. Thomas Jefferson's interest in classical Roman design, as evidenced by his home Monticello, built at the end of the eighteenth century, provided a logical step to an interest in Greek architecture.

Houses in the preceding Georgian style, with their high, gabled roofs and symmetrical layout, could be made classical by turning the gabled end toward the street and adding a columned portico. Greek Revival incorporated straight lines with modest embellishments. During this period, 1820–1860, people became familiar with architectural terms like Ionic, Doric, and Corinthian columns, pediments, and entablatures, all components of classic Greek architecture.

Left: Built by San Franciscan architect Henry W. Cleveland between 1865–68, this 26 room Italian villa shows wonderful balance and grace from the top of its open arched cupola, to its pronounced, second floor window pediments.

Benjamin Asher's *Pattern Books of American Classical Architecture,* and Minard Lafever's Greek Revival pattern book, *Beauties of Modern Architecture,* helped spread these designs across the country, providing a starting point for many carpenter builders.

The best known example of Greek Revival style, done on a grand scale, is the American Southern plantation house, with its broad expanse of columns and simple lines, all painted stark white. Fortunately, many of these survived the Civil War. In New York City, Alexander Jackson Davis, thought by some to be one of the most creative architects of the era, designed luxurious marble townhouses, with colonnade fronts that echoed the same Greek origin.

Greek Revival style homes were also evident in other parts of the country, in the form of small, one-story frame, or two-story brick houses. If the homeowner was unable to afford an expanse of columned porch, the house might feature only a small portico over the entrance, with pilasters at either side to simulate columns. The typical, front-gabled farmhouse pays homage to Greek Revival style.

Greek Revival served as more than just an architectural model, it was also a symbol of a new democracy and a breaking away from the old. Gothic Revival and the other "revivals" that followed had a symbolic aspect as well. Rather than mere architectural replicas, like earlier Georgian and Federalist houses, the "revivals" stood for something or evoked a spirit from the period which they represented, and so were characterized as part of the Romantic Movement.

In the following decades, house designs incorporated several architectural styles, all of them imitative of historic European models. The past was idealized and traits such as spontaneity and individualism, that seemed to go hand-in-hand with freedom, were valued. The arts in general reflected this interest in romanticism in the novels of Sir Walter Scott, James Fenimore Cooper, the Brontë sisters, the music of Franz Liszt and Frederic Chopin, and the poetry of Baudelaire.

The Gothic Revival style house with its tall peaks and pointed arches of its entryways and narrow windows, reflected a romantic return to the age of chivalry, coupled with a Christian piety. Richard Upjohn, an English-born draftsman, was in part responsible for introducing this style to the United States and Andrew Jackson Downing is credited with spreading designs for Gothic Revival homes with his book *The Architecture of Country Houses.*

Gothic Revival was largely popular around 1840–1880, principally on the East Coast, but also in the Midwest. The decorative vergeboard or bargeboard trim (plain or intricately cut boards that outline a gable) presaged the trend of extravagant gingerbread. Some houses featured square towers, reminiscent of medieval castles. The typical material was board and batten siding, vertical boards covering the surface of the house, accented by vertical wooden strips where the boards joined. Because of their projection, the battens would cast shadows providing an interesting rhythmical effect. Trim work and tracery designs that emulated stonework done in previous centuries, were medieval in character and were also repeated in the interiors.

A plain, Federalist or Greek Revival style home could be made contemporary by applying cutouts of fanciful wooden trim. A well known example is the Wedding Cake House in Kennebunk, Maine, a 1825 Federal style home with an elaborate Gothic "frosting" of pinnacled buttresses covering it.

After the 1830s, many new houses were of balloon frame construction rather than beam and post timber. This speedy method of framing a house allowed for greater variation in room sizes and shapes, and

Right, above: *This 1880s home of G.W. Patterson is a classic Queen Anne, distinguished by its arched entryway and balcony, rounded porch, and tower topped by a witch's cap, and decorated gable.*

Right, below: *Home to the family of John Alfred Kimberly of the Kimberly-Clark Corporation, this mansion is an example of the Chateauesque or French Renaissance style, conceived by Richard Morris Hunt.*

Left, above: This pretty little 1882 Gothic Revival or Carpenter Gothic, built by easterner William Kelly—founder of Mendocino, California—shows how eastern styles were transferred to the West Coast.

Left, below: Delicate and fanciful are the words that come to mind for this 1886 Queen Anne cottage. Built on a lake in Arcadia, Pasadena, and designed by architect Albert A. Bennett, it combines Stick and Eastlake detailing in an imaginative and pleasing manner.

Below: This 1892 Queen Anne called Heritage House, in Riverside, California, seems top heavy because of the second floor projection and the rather squat domed turret. The shingle decoration and decorative tracery work on the windows help to lighten the overall effect.

asymmetry in design. Thanks to new steam-powered sawmills that churned out the lightweight lumber used in balloon framing, and other machinery that automated what had formerly been artisan crafts, the working family could afford a version of a Gothic Revival house, dubbed Gothic Carpenter, because they were designed by carpenter builders. Examples of these picturesque houses can still be seen in the countryside and small towns of the United States and Canada.

Existing concurrently with the Gothic Revival home was the Italianate, which made its way out to the northern coast of California and was popular in the Midwest. In contrast to the sharply-pitched roofs of the Gothic Revival, Italianate homes had low-pitched or flat roofs. Decorative supportive brackets under large eaves and cupolas were other architectural features of this style.

An Italianate home could range from the imitation of a simple Italian farmhouse with little ornamentation, to High Italianate with square towers topped by cupolas, large cornice brackets, and entry porches. Like the Gothic Revival, this style also featured tall windows, but with rounded tops, versus the pointed Gothic arch

A citified version of Italianate, clean and elegant, but strictly for the well-to-do, was the Renaissance Revival style that emphasized formalism along with symmetrical, early sixteenth century Italian elements. Built exclusively of stone or brick, it featured accents of rusticated quoins (accents, usually of contrasting color or material on corners of buildings), and doors with entablatures or pediments.

France made its contribution to North American Victorian architecture with the mansard roof, popular on homes following the Second Empire style. The mansard roof, created by French architect François Mansart to circumvent Paris building codes and taxes, allowed a full story to exist under the eaves. Dormer windows ringed these roofs, that were often covered with colored tile work or shingles and topped by decorative ironwork. Not all Second Empire houses had mansard roofs; other architectural details could include contrasting colors for belt courses, quoins, overhangs, and brackets (but smaller than those on Italianate homes), a projecting central pavilion that was higher than the rest of the house, and tall, first floor, sometimes paired, windows.

Second Empire was so named after the reign of Napoleon III, during which a massive building effort took place in Paris. It flourished as an urban style because it was ideal for narrow lots. The generous use of bay windows let in plenty of light. It was a style found mainly in the Northeast and Midwest from 1855–1885, though its decline began with the 1873 financial panic and following depression that put a hold on new house construction.

Right: *The Whittier mansion. This Richardsonian Romanesque was built wired for electricity in 1896, before it was commonly used in the home. Architect Edward Swain gave the San Fransican mansion an inside as imposing as the exterior.*

Left: *An exemplary illustration of the Southern plantation interpretation of Greek Revival and Italianate, this 1855 mansion in Natchez, called Dunleith, features a Tuscan portico of two-story columns, hipped roof, dentil trim along the eaves and cast-iron railings.*

Left, above: *Designed by Henry Dudley, a prolific New York architect of the popular firm of Diaper and Dudley, the 1865 Park-McCullough House in North Bennington, Vermont, features a Second Empire design, as evidenced by the mansard roof. Notice the narrow, rounded, top windows and delicate porch columns with ornamented brackets.*

Left, below: *The 1864 Lockwood-Mathews mansion in Norwalk, Connecticut is High Victorian, marked by its elegant, rounded porch supported by slim columns, wrought-iron work on the balconies and roof, and combination of mansard and gabled roofs.*

Above: *Shingles cover the unusual shapes of this Queen Anne built in 1887 in San Diego for musician Jesse Shepard. Stained-glass windows, raised foundation, dentils along the roofline, a potted chimney, and Turkish dome topped tower all contribute to the exotic flavor of Villa Montezuma.*

You won't see many of them, but when you do, you'll know it immediately. The octagon house was created to emulate nature's sphere, creating more space with less structure. In 1853, Orson Fowler wrote *The Octagon House: a Home for All* to sing the praises of this unique design, which he promoted as providing more sunlight, heat, and better ventilation, due in part to its lack of real corners. His advocacy of indoor water closets and hot air furnaces was ahead of his time.

Besides the distinction of being eight-sided, other architectural features were cupolas, hipped or low-pitched roofs, and raised basements. The octagon craze lasted from approximately 1853–1870, and a number of these structures are scattered throughout the country today.

Above: Called Nutt's Folly by the locals, Longwood is described as the largest octagonal house in America, though it was never completed. Designed by Philadelphia architect Samuel Sloan for physician Haller Nutt and his family, the house was to have been six stories containing 32 rooms. Work was halted in 1861 by the outbreak of the Civil War. The sixteen-sided cupola, large bracketed roof overhangs, and porches with their delicate columns show how the Italianate style worked perfectly with the octagonal.

Right: More popular west of the Mississippi, the Queen Anne style epitomized the eclectic nature of architecture and furnishings that permeated the Victorian era. Typical are the turret, expansive porch or veranda, and the Eastlake spindle work decorating the porch roof. The cone-shaped roofs on the porch and the octagonal one atop the house's bay window, both crowned by finials, add to the free spirit of the 1896 Pillow-Thompson House in Helena, Arkansas.

The Stick style is also easily recognizable, in this case by the myriad of vertical, diagonal, and horizontal wooden pieces, or sticks, on the surface of the exterior, giving the home a timbered or Tudor effect. The steeply pitched roofs hearken back to the Gothic Revival and some referred to Stick style as High Victorian Gothic, while others called it an extension of Carpenter Gothic. Architect Richard Morris Hunt helped popularize the style with his designs of vacation houses for the rich in Newport, Rhode Island, around 1870. Houses that had additional decorative trim were called Stick-Eastlake, after the English architect and writer Charles Eastlake.

Charles Eastlake had immeasurable influence on the tastes and designs of homes and furniture in the last quarter of the century. In his widely read *Hints on Household Taste in Furniture, Upholstery and Other Details*, he advocated simplicity versus ornateness, and artisan craftsmanship versus poorly manufactured, mass-produced designs.

Embellishments added to trusses, porches with decorative supports, a lot of spindle work, and dormers with wide overhangs made Stick and Stick-Eastlake one of the quintessential Victorian architectures. The detailing is reminiscent of rustic European architecture such as Swiss chalets or Tudor cottages. A significant contribution of these styles was the introduction of color into the Victorian landscape. Some of the color combinations, maroon walls, dark green trim, deep reddish orange window sashes, and olive brown blinds or shutters, sound a trifle odd to us today.

Almon Varney in his 1885 *Our Homes and Their Adornments* had this advice, "Every house should have two or more tints; the cornice and verandas should be of a contrasting shade with the body of the house, while the shutters, etc. should have a darker tint than either. Of the various colors, the olive tints in their different shades are very pleasing to the eye, also lavender, drabs, stone, etc. A pea-green is a very healthful color, and with proper contrasts in veranda and shutters is very pleasing."

In San Francisco, California, between 1850–1915, 48,000 homes were built, many of them in the Stick-Eastlake style. The 1885

Above: *Painted brick, red, cream, maroon, and green to duplicate the original palette, this 15 room Arkansas home was built in 1883 by J.W. Hill for $17,000.*

Left, above: *The 1850 San Francisco Plantation near Reserve, Louisiana, features a severely recessed porch and bracketed roof, typical of Italianate style, but the freestanding turret with onion style dome adds an exotic Turkish element.*

Left, below: *The mansard roof with its hooded windows and the tall central pavilion are elements of Italianate Second Empire in Terrace Hill, a home that is now the Iowa's governor's residence. Designed by Chicago architect William Boyington, it was called the "finest residence west of the Hudson River" when it was built in 1869. Note the stone decoration on the corners, called quoins, which provide contrast and decoration to the façade.*

California Architects and Builders News described the homes as "using more colors by far than the tailor who designed Joseph's coat." Today only about 16,000 of these homes remain. After passing through a drab period when their "coats of many colors" were covered with gray and white paint, they again are brilliantly vibrant, thanks to the Colorist movement of the 1960s.

Another outstanding feature of Stick-Eastlake is that the interior details reflected the exterior architecture, giving it a structural integrity not found in some of the other styles. Many summer homes built by the wealthy favored the Stick style for its informality and rustic appearance. It flourished near the end of the century, 1860–1890, in the Northeast and Northwest.

Romanesque Revival is synonymous with Richardsonian Romanesque, after Henry Hobson Richardson, the second American (Richard Morris Hunt was the first), to attend the Ecole des Beaux Arts in Paris. Although Romanesque buildings were mainly public ones, because they were built exclusively of stone and expressed a permanence associated with municipal buildings, churches, libraries, etc., some of the very rich commissioned these palatial or chateau-like houses, which had, at the same time, a rustic air to them.

Popular from around 1870–1900, the effect depended on mass, volume, and scale rather than decorative features. Transomed windows in groups or rows set into the wall, arched entries without columns, short towers, and chimneys to emphasize the solid shape of the building, broad hip roofs with eaves close to the wall, were all components of Richardsonian Romanesque. Actually, Richardson himself designed very few of these houses, most are copies.

In the last quarter of the century came what might be called the pièce de resistance of Victorian architecture, the Queen Anne style. The Queen Anne had it all, turrets, towers, domes, bay windows, multiple planes, projections and overhangs, verandas, and balconies, all accompanied by decorative trim and sometimes riotous color. When the economy began its rebound, after the 1873 financial panic, new home builders wanted a new house fashion and the Queen Anne was it.

British architect Norman Shaw first used the style in England. The name Queen Anne is confusing because the elements defining the style have little to do with the Queen Anne period. In Shaw's creation of a new style he advocated a return to two historical periods, the folk buildings with half-timbered walls of the Middle Ages, and the symmetrical Renaissance designs popular during the 1702–14 reign of Queen Anne. Although it was the half-timbered motif that was adopted by American architects, it was dubbed Queen Anne.

Awareness of the style in America was created by a book of his sketches that was published in 1858, and more so by his drawings that were published in periodicals here and in England. At the 1876 Philadelphia Centennial Exposition, American architects saw models of the Queen Anne style and embraced it wholeheartedly.

Architects in this country were inspired by Shaw's ideas and felt free to expand and embellish them to match the ebullient spirit of the century's end. The emphasis in Queen Anne style was on fancifulness and exuberance. The varying projections and shapes, the combination of exterior finishes, stone or brick on one story, clapboard, stucco or shingles on another, combined with decorative elements of stained glass, tiled chimneys, finials, and crests on roofs, all made it the perfect style for expressing one's individuality.

***

Right, above: *The owner of this 1892 Flemish Renaissance mansion, brewer Frederick Pabst, led a movement against Victorian Gothic and Eastlake style at the 1893 Chicago World Colombian Exposition. A proponent of the Aesthetic Movement, he contracted architect George Bowman Ferry to design this dignified home of pressed brick with terra cotta ornament.*

Right, below: *This home of Ulysses S. Grant, dating from 1865, is a wonderful example of Italianate in its purest form. Made of brick with a flat roof, wide, bracketed eaves, and small columned entrance topped by a balcony, it presents classic elements of this style.*

Like the Stick style houses, some of whose elements are used on Queen Annes, the Queen Anne was painted in a riot of colors, if subdued ones. Earth tones such as sienna, hunter green, and ocher were the colors of the era.

Next to the Shingle style, which was strictly an American creation, the Queen Anne was considered the most American of the Victorian period architectures, because innovations carried it far beyond its roots. Popular from 1880–1910, it was one of the few styles that made its way to the South, as well as to the West Coast.

At the very end of the century, 1880–1900, came the aforementioned Shingle style, considered to be strictly American conceived. As the name implies, the house was covered by shingles. Like the Stick style, Shingle houses were first built as vacation homes for the wealthy, because of their rustic air. Ample and numerous porches also made them suitable as summer homes. This house style stayed mainly on the eastern seaboard, though examples can be found in the Midwest.

Perhaps the most common of all surviving Victorian era homes is the Folk Victorian, of which the Carpenter Gothic is an example. Folk Victorians were built by carpenters, not architects, and often combined elements from various architectural styles, but minus the large bay windows, turrets, and balconies that characterized the larger homes of the wealthy. In general, the elements are from Gothic Revival, Stick or Queen Anne styles, and were built throughout most of the Victorian period and throughout most of North America. In true Victorian style they were built to the owner's taste. "Sufficient it is now to say that uniformity is the last thing on earth to be sought for in different homes, either outwardly or inwardly, just as it is in persons," advised a 1898 *House Beautiful* article titled "Individuality in Homes."

The era ended as it began with a return to classicism. The 1876 Centennial Exposition introduced the Colonial Revival style in some of its exhibition buildings. The following year noted architects McKim, Mead, White, and Bigelow, toured the eastern coast looking at original homes built during the Federal and Georgian periods in the 1700s, before designing two notable houses in Colonial Revival style. Featuring a restrained classical manner with columns and symmetry as the main architectural features, Colonial Revival has lasted up to this day.

In a parallel turn toward simplicity, tenets of the Arts and Crafts Movement affected the whole of the living environment from the outside to the inside, to furniture and garden design. The Arts and Crafts Movement grew out of the Aesthetic Movement, begun in England by John Ruskin, which proposed that home design should express one's character or individuality, versus the earlier Victorian notion that the home's purpose was to shape individual and national character.

In this vein, the Arts and Crafts Movement was about a return to nature and local building traditions with local materials, about handmade versus machine-made. Although it was late in the century when this movement gained momentum, it evolved into the Craftsman style that lasted well into the twentieth century.

Left: The mansard roof and pavilion projecting beyond the roof line cry out Second Empire. However, the trio of windows, rounded archway of the door and colonnaded porch add a touch of the Italianate, in the 1864 Morris-Butler House in Indianapolis. A Queen Anne style porch was added in 1892.

The Victorian Parlor

The word "parlor" belongs to the Victorian period. Sitting room, drawing room, living room are all synonyms, but it is only the word "parlor" that is synonymous with the Victorians. That is quite fitting as, for the Victorians, the parlor, or parlor life, represented the most important aspects of Victorian life.

Says Louise Stevenson in *The Victorian Homefront, American Thought and Culture, 1860–1880*, "Victorians wouldn't have been Victorians without their parlors. Here families assembled, met their guests and entertained themselves and others through conversation, playing games, putting on plays, viewing stereographs, singing and enjoying music, writing letters, and engaging in the paramount parlor activity, reading."

Parlors ranged from the simple front room with its center table before the fireplace, topped by a family Bible, to the multi-purposed rooms in the houses of the well-to-do, where different functions of the parlor had separate spaces devoted to them.

In the mid-nineteenth century, as American society changed from agrarian to industrial, and individualism began to assert itself, home life became paramount. The love of the family, the love between husbands and wives, and above all, a mother's love for her children, were felt to be an extension of God's love, and therefore home was a "little heaven on earth."

So it was to the parlor, the center of that home, that Victorians directed their best efforts at decorating and at self-expression. The center table, whether left bare or covered by a fringed cloth, depending on the fashion at the time, was the most important piece of furniture. It was around this table that the family gathered to read, to sew, to play games—to relax, in other words. Lighting was a kerosene or oil lamp on the table, or hung above it. Some speculated that the table was originally placed in the center of the room to be under the center-hung light and so prevent people from hitting their heads.

Beyond the center table and the chairs gathered around it, early Victorians didn't think about how furniture might be pleasingly arranged or how to accessorize their room that represented them to others, until they caught glimpses of "model parlors," parlors in hotels, steamboats, and railroad cars. The 1876 Centennial Exposition in Philadelphia is credited with exposing its visitors to sample parlors. It wasn't until later in the century that furniture stores began to display their wares in "sample rooms." Other ideas about parlor décor were gleaned from contact with the English gentry here, and visits abroad. The French were always to be imitated.

From about 1857, the middle class could purchase parlor furniture in suites. The rich had long had the option of custom-designed rooms of furniture. A seven-piece suite,

Left: Stained-glass windows were a feature of the Victorian era, first as an imitation of Gothic Revival architectural elements then later when John La Farge began creating stained-glass designs in the United States. A gaming table with furniture in the Eastlake style is well-placed to receive natural light.

consisting of a sofa, upholstered armchair (for the man), an upholstered armless, or ladies' chair, and four smaller chairs with upholstered seats and backs was the norm. Consumers could select from furniture catalogs by the 1870s.

Rosewood, mahogany, maple, and oak were popular woods used in furniture. Upholstery was from a variety of fabrics such as satin damask, velvet, plush, or the more economical horsehair. Parlor sofas with sides that curved inward, or "S" shaped sofas in which the occupants sat in opposing directions allowing them to face one another, were both known as *têtes à têtes* or just *têtes* for short.

Furniture styles ranged from the Gothic Revival, prior to 1850, characterized by squarish, medieval looking designs to Rococo Revival and Louis XVI Revival. The golden oak movement at the end of the century lightened up and relieved Victorian décor of some of its fussiness.

Cabinetmaker John Henry Belter opened a furniture shop in New York City where he produced a highly successful line of furniture in the curved, Louis XV manner. Balloon-shaped chair and sofa backs with curving edges and detailed carving, mark his creations, which he made from 1844 until his death in 1863.

Charles Eastlake ranted against the "extravagance of contour" in sofas and chairs as, "[insuring] the greatest amount of ugliness with the least possible comfort." He admonished, "A curve at the back of a sofa means nothing at all, and is manifestly inconvenient, for it must render it either too high in one place or too low in another to accommodate the shoulders of a sitter."

Though he never designed furniture, his ideas about simplicity of design and handcrafted versus poorly made manufactured pieces, led to an Eastlake style of furniture, that, ironically enough, was taken up and misinterpreted by the "ignorant mechanics" he condemned.

How "ignorant" the "mechanics" were is debatable for the business of manufactured furniture, as exemplified by companies in Grand Rapids, Michigan, and Cincinnati, Ohio, was one of the results of the mechanization of the Industrial Revolution. While much of manufactured furniture was of poor quality, some businesses hired artists and craftsmen from Europe to help translate the aesthetics of handmade furniture into the mass-produced, available for all.

Right: above: *The Queen Anne style chairs by the window, combine with Turkish style* têtes *and ladies' chairs to tastefully decorate the ladies' parlor in the Park-McCullough House. Ladies' chairs were intentionally armless to accommodate the full-skirted fashions.*

Right, below: *A cozy invitation to tea is ready in the rear, or family, parlor of Harriet Beecher Stowe's house in Hartford, Connecticut. The violet patterned tea set was designed by Stowe and manufactured by the Minton Company. Note the replica of* Venus de Milo *between the windows.*

Left: *This smoking room in the 1896 Whittier mansion is what was known as a Turkish "cozy corner." The mahogany and white oak woodwork, oriental rugs, and Turkish motif make this a luxurious nook for the man of the house.*

Parlor accoutrements were often a piano or organ (for those not wealthy enough to have a separate music room), other tables, marble-topped if the pocketbook allowed, for displaying works of art, photo albums, and travel mementos. Until the Arts and Crafts Movement at the end of the century counteracted the excesses of Victorian décor with the suggestion that austerity would be the new theme, fabric was everywhere, outside the usual bounds of window covering and upholstery. "Tidies," small pieces of lace or embroidered fabric, covered chair backs to prevent soil from hair-oil staining the material. Mantels, tables, and shelves, in addition to windows, were covered by lambrequins.

Lambrequins, a fancy word from the French meaning decorative drapery, were made of embroidered fabric, chintz, or of fringed damask. A lambrequin atop a window was used to hide the workings of the drapery, much like a valance is today. Lace was also heavily used on windows to soften the glare and to provide a pleasing contrast to the heavier velvet or damask curtains.

Curtains called *portieres* (again, the French influence), were also used to cover doors, as ornamentation when draped around the doorway, and to eliminate drafts when hung loose to cover the closed door or entranceway. Sometimes more than a dozen patterns, between wallpaper, carpet, lambrequins, and curtains, were combined in the Victorian parlor, helping to create the notion we have today of Victorian clutter.

Whether the parlor contained an organ or piano depended on the family's religious and social aspirations. A parlor organ, as an accompaniment to hymn singing, enabled the family to incorporate more religious experience into the home life. The piano, on the other hand, was more historically linked to

Above: *Here is the drawing room in Samuel Clemen's house. The silver stenciling on the doors and walls, echoing motifs from American Indian, East Indian, and African designs, is a restoration of the original by Louis Comfort Tiffany. An Oriental influence is also reflected in the large vases on either side of the fireplace.*

Left, above: *Rococo Revival and French influence weigh heavily in the sitting rooms of this early Natchez, Mississippi, mansion named Melrose. Fluted Ionic columns frame sliding doors at the back of the room. The formal furniture, probably from New York or Philadelphia, seems more for perching than for sitting. The oil burning chandelier, drapery, and cornices are original to the house.*

Left, below: *The columns and dentil-decorated frieze of this 1844 interior show a Greek Revival influence. The concealed doors of this double room separate the visiting parlor from the music room to the rear.*

European culture, and therefore more of a status symbol. By mid-century pianos began to be mass-produced and were affordable by the middle class.

In larger homes, a separate room was devoted to music and guests were invited specifically for the purpose of enjoying an evening of musical entertainment. Piano or organ playing was an ability encouraged in women especially, and listening to a performance on the parlor piano was as pervasive then as watching television is now.

Wall and floor treatment varied according to decade. In the 1830s and 40s, wall treatment tended to be plain painted walls in light colors, or imported wallpaper for those who could afford it. Later in the century, after 1870, proper Victorian taste dictated a wall divided into three parts: the lower three feet or dado, covered by wood wainscoting or wallpaper, the middle section or field, painted, and the top part near the ceiling, or frieze, papered, or decorated with a stenciled border.

Wallpaper became more affordable once it was printed on roller presses in the 1850s instead of block-printed. Patterns ranged from simple filigree, garland, or floral designs to geometric and Oriental-influenced designs later in the period. Embossed leather, Lincrusta, a linseed oil composition, and Anagylta, made of

Above: This parlor has been restored to its original appearance as part of Old Wade House, a 1851 inn on the plank road between Sheboygan and Fond du Lac, Wisconsin. The cloth-covered center table and organ are typical elements of the early Victorian era parlor.

Right: The Turkish sitting room of Château-sur-Mer, furnished in 1890s Oriental style, exemplifies the excess associated with the "typical" Victorian décor. The fringed furniture, fringed lambrequin covering the bric-a-brac-topped mantel, and riot of patterns and colors all add to the effect.

Left: This white marble fireplace in the sitting room of Terrace Hill is one of eight in the house. The lace curtain insets and Madonna and Child painting, reflected in the mirror, are pure Victorian.

Right: The Roycroft furniture in this parlor is an example of the Arts and Crafts Movement that counteracted some of the frou-frou of the later Victorian period. Named after the seventeenth century printers Samuel and Thomas Roycroft, the furniture exemplified handcraftsmanship in its use of pegs with mortise and tenon joints.

Below: A unique feature of this family parlor in the Honolulu House in Marshall, Michigan, is the twin slate fireplaces painted to look like marble. Using painting techniques to imitate wood and marble was common during the Victorian era.

cotton pulp, were also used as wall covering. Although décor mavens dictated a decorated (i.e, papered) ceiling complete with cornices, the more common choice was plain white. For walls, popular colors were strong ones such as crimson, plum, dark greens, and blues, until the end of the century when taste turned again to pastel colors.

In the earlier part of the century, floors were typically made of pine and therefore, more likely to be covered with wall-to-wall carpeting. Hardwood floors were not machine-made until the 1870s, at which time they became popular (i.e., affordable), with the middle class. Wooden floors were the norm, covered by rugs and carpets. Wall-to-wall carpeting, not as we know it today, was made in widths of 27 inches then handstitched together to create room-sized carpets. Axminster and Wilton were two popular British manufacturers of patterned carpeting and by the end of the century, Oriental rugs were status symbols.

World politics at the time contributed to accessorizing the Victorian parlor. Britain's strong imperial policy under Queen Victoria created colonies in South Africa, Egypt, and India. The British translated some of their worldly experiences into home décor which were eagerly copied across the pond. The United States promoted its own brand of imperialism against Native American people as the West was opened, and against Mexico and Panama. One result of these "incursions" was to introduce indigenous patterns and objects into the Victorian home.

These exotic motifs could either reinforce the generally cluttered air of the parlor or, in the eyes of Eastlake, be uplifting. "It is impossible to overrate the influence which such objects may have in educating the eye to appreciate what really constitutes good art. An Indian ginger-jar, a Flemish beer-jug, a Japanese fan, may each become, in turn, a valuable lesson in decorative form and color."

Left: *The drawing room in the Cape May Mainstay Inn displays a beautifully upholstered* tête a tête *in the foreground combined with pieces of Renaissance and Rococo Revival furniture. The drapery design shows a Turkish influence while the wallpaper has a classical pattern.*

Right: *Even a large, Rococo Revival style parlor had its center table, small though it be. A number of art objects adorn this elaborate parlor in the Morris-Butler House with its furniture in the style of John Henry Belter.*

The Victorian Dining Room

It's safe to say that the second most important room in the Victorian home was the dining room, where not only the family gathered, but where social interaction took place among family and visitors. "In the family it should be observed as a rule to meet together at all meals of the day around one common table where the same rules of etiquette should be as rigidly observed as at the table of a stranger," said Almon Varney in his *Our Homes and Their Adornments*.

Up to the Elizabethan period, no one room was specifically designated for eating. Meals took place in sitting rooms, kitchens, or hall/entrance ways (which were sizable) in which tables and chairs, or benches, were set up for meals, then removed afterward. Grand mansions, of course, had their banquet halls. It was when a room convenient to the kitchen and pantry evolved, that the dining room, as we know it, came to be.

Above: *Painted woodwork and light colored wallpaper give a light and airy effect that was more typical of the early Victorian period, and of the California region. The milk glass fruit basket, sheer curtains, and white marble fireplace contribute to this California style room.*

Left: *This wooden coffered ceiling is unusual for a dining room. However, in the Haas-Lilienthal House in San Francisco, it is nicely matched by the original furnishing of an Eastlake style fireplace mantel, dining table, and chairs of the Renaissance Revival era.*

Left, above: Victorians were big on celebrating holidays as this egg decorated table indicates. In this 1886 farmhouse the furnishings are simple and the wall and floor décor make a cozy, appealing room.

Left, below: Set for a buffet russe, the table in this dining room displays the variety of china and silver that accompanied Victorian meals. The tile-covered fireplace is decorated for harvest, and the mantel, with its tiers of shelves, is a place to display serving pieces in lieu of a grand sideboard.

Right, above: Done in 1903–1905 by the Boston architectural firm of Shepley, Rutan, and Coolidge, the Hildene House dining room illustrates the interest in Colonial Revival at the end of the Victorian period. The wooden wainscoting and frieze of the walls, coupled with wallpaper depicting a country scene, provide a restful setting for a meal. The Queen Anne furniture completes the simple and elegant effect of this post-Victorian dining room. Note the table is unclothed.

Right, below: The simple dining room of this roadside inn known as Wade House expresses the same hospitality as that of its fancier neighbors. The plank table, plain wooden chairs, and lantern-like ceiling fixtures invite the guests to a hearty home-cooked meal.

Dining rooms were also public rooms in which the best in furniture and décor was displayed. Typical dining room furniture would be a table, if possible with extensions (an invention that occurred during the Victorian period), dining chairs, and a sideboard or chiffonier for storing serving pieces and presenting food.

During this period, dining rose to its most elegant state. Etiquette books prescribed serving and dining behavior down to the smallest detail. Serving pieces and dining utensils had very specific purposes such as pickle casters with pickle tongs, celery dishes, and syllabub-sticks.

Sideboards made of walnut, oak, or mahogany could include features like carved columns and friezes, pediments, and cornices, and were small works of architecture in themselves. Styles ranged from the intricately carved Jacobean and Gothic or Rococo Revival, to the clean lines of a Sheraton or Chippendale piece.

Beginning around the 1860s, the sideboard was the most important piece of furniture in the dining room, equal in relevance to the parlor's center table. Families with sufficient means had built in sideboards. An 1892 *Ladies Home Journal* article tells what the sideboard is for, "Several people have asked me about the uses of the sideboard. The drawers are for the silver and cutlery, the closets for wine, if they be used, and often for such things as preserved ginger, confectionery, cut sugar, and indeed, any of the many little things that one

Above: *Near the end of the nineteenth century, dark mahogany, cherry, and walnut woods were replaced by a lighter look, as typified by this golden oak wainscoting and furniture. The handsome dining room set follows the simple lines advocated by Charles Eastlake. This color scheme of red and gold was considered passé by the end of the Victorian period.*

Left: *The Louis XV furnishings and woodwork in this Pabst mansion dining room are attributed to Matthews Bros., Milwaukee cabinetmakers. The chandelier can be fueled by kerosene, gas, or electricity. The shell motifs on the ceiling are reminiscent of Renaissance decorative patterns.*

likes to have in the dining-room yet out of sight. The water pitcher and other silver and pretty bits of china can be placed on the sideboard. Cracker jar and fruit dish also belong there. At dinner time the dessert dishes are usually arranged upon it."

The dining room table had been a relatively simple piece of furniture up to mid-century, when the extension table became popular. Drop-leaf and gate-leg tables preceded the extension table, as ways to increase the size of the dining area when needed. Author and arbiter of taste, Edith Wharton, was not partial to the idea. "The ingenious but ugly extension-table with a central support, now used all over the world, is an English invention. There seems to be no reason why the general design should not be improved without interfering with the mechanism of this table; but of course it can never be so satisfactory to the eye as one of the old round or square tables with four or six tapering legs, such as were used in the eighteenth-century dining rooms before the introduction of the 'extension'."

Outside of the simple country table or one designed by Sheraton or Heppelwhite, the dining room table was an extraordinarily massive piece of furniture with, depending on the exact style, fluted columns, clawed feet, or pedestal bases. Earlier in the century, the lines of the popular Renaissance Revival demanded very tall sideboards and high backed chairs, while later, the graceful lines of the Art Nouveau and lower profile Arts and Crafts Movement, presented a more horizontal effect. It was recommended that the chairs around the dining table be of material that was easily cleaned such as cane, or leather, if upholstery was absolutely essential.

Wall and floor decoration followed the patterns of other rooms in the house, according to the period. Dining rooms from the 1840s and 1850s had plain painted walls and not much in the way of wall decoration. Then came the deeply shaded walls of crimson, gold, or deep green or blue. Wainscoting or even fully paneled walls added an elegant touch. Lincrusta, an embossed wallpaper of a composition material that could be easily cleaned, was popular as a dado treatment for adding texture to the wall.

Area rugs were used throughout the century in the dining room. Wood floors were noisy but wall-to-wall carpeting harbored odors and food stains. Of course, it could be protected by laying a crumb cloth underneath the table. After 1880, wood parquet floors in a variety of patterns provided an option to the pine planks or oak-wood strips of earlier homes.

The intent, maybe more so in the dining room than parlor, was to create an atmosphere of comfort that was also functional. Above all, good taste must be observed, for it was all too easy to slip from a refined display of china, glass, and silver, to an ostentatious showiness of excessive material goods.

Dinner parties were elaborate, starting with engraved invitations. There was great discourse on how many tablecloths to use, two or three (removed in stages between courses). Courses were numerous, starting with soup, followed by fish, then game, or other meat. Vegetables accompanied the meat, then came a salad course. Finger bowls were used, dessert and a fruit course concluded the meal, and coffee was served, either at the table or in the parlor or library. At this point, the sexes might separate if the men were to indulge in smoking and brandies.

Right, above: Here at Copshalolm, an impressive display of wood tastefully reveals the status of the home owner. The Chippendale table, sideboard, and chairs, along with lead glass cabinet doors and, of course, the beamed and decoratively papered ceiling, give this room the feel of a rich man's club.

Right, below: A Victorian table laid out for a formal dinner gives an idea of the intricacies involved in dining. This oddly shaped room, an alcove at the end sheltering the altar-like sideboard, is filled perfectly by this table for twelve. Note the beautiful pediments above the windows.

The Victorian Bedroom

Bedroom fashions changed dramatically over the Victorian years due to several factors. Early in the period, homes were heated by fireplaces and therefore could be uncomfortable in the colder months, although a heated bedroom was considered an indulgence and windows were left open even during the winter. In reality, only the rich had fireplaces in their bedrooms.

Still, one had to keep warm while asleep and bed drapery, consisting variously of canopies, tents, and other enclosures used to shut out drafts, was essential, as was heavy drapery on windows. Even doors had decorative, but also functional, drapes called *portieres* that served to keep out drafts when covering the door.

By the end of the century, two things had changed that affected bedroom styles. First, coal and woodburning parlor stoves came into use, were more efficient at heating a house, and could be installed in any room. (Central heating, though available after the Civil War, was really only for the very rich.) Secondly, and more importantly, was an increased knowledge of diseases, germs, and bacteria and how to combat them. Plenty of fresh air with good circulation, and the elimination of materials such as bed drapery that not only impeded air circulation but provided a place for dust and bacteria to collect were

Above: The Colonial Ropes mansion in Salem, Massachusetts, is refurbished with 1890s reproductions. A dominating bed is softened by the wicker chair and basket and a kilim rug and small-figured wallpaper add homey touches. The cheval glass on the dresser was very typical of bedroom furniture of this period.

Left: The Eastlake style is evident in the bedstead of this High Victorian room. The stained-glass windows and plants on their Rococo Revival stands give the room a rather exotic air. What appears to be a chamber pot is next to the bed, though the house had a bathroom.

Above: Every element of a mid-to-late century Victorian bedroom is in this crowded room at Chateau-sur-Mer. The writing desk and chair are oddly placed at the foot of the Renaissance Revival bed. A chaise in the right hand corner invites lounging and a decorative screen hides the washstand in the far right corner. The fireplace has an insert for more effective heating.

Below: This is the bedroom at Dunsmuir House, California, which was built by Alexander Dunsmuir for his new wife Josephine Wallace, his patient mistress of twenty years standing. The rattan bedstead, brass tray topped table, and American Indian rug show influences from around the world, typical of the late Victorian period.

Above: Cozy is the word that comes to mind to describe this room under the eaves. The modest bed is surrounded by a dressing table and mirror and table and chair by the window, for reading with good light. The light colors and airy curtains provide a healthful look to this 1873 bedroom.

Below: The mammoth headboard of this Renaissance Gothic style bed dwarfs the other furniture in this room. The patterned carpet, the only kind available during the Victorian era, has no competing element in the wallpaper. The simplicity, despite the elaborate bed, is befitting a California ranch where this is one of 26 rooms.

deemed essential. Since the bedroom served as the place where daily and weekly ablutions were performed (until bathrooms became separate entities), and as a birthing and maternity room, it was important that it have a healthy environment.

Styles of bedroom furniture were affected by this new found interest in and concern for prevention of illness and diseases. The classic English styles of Sheraton, Chippendale, and Hepplewhite migrated from the eighteenth century into the Victorian period. Tall, four-poster canopied beds enclosed the sleeper in heavy drapes of wool or lined damask or velvet, a carryover from the time when houses were built without corridors, and enclosures around the bed were needed for privacy, as well as warmth.

By the time mid-century had arrived, the full enclosure had receded to the half-tester, or half-canopy, from which hung draperies that covered only the head and shoulders. Fully enclosed beds were now considered unhygienic, as they limited air circulation and the yards of fabric attracted dust. Dust ruffles and window valances were also discarded in the same house cleaning. In the southern climates, netting was still necessary to protect against insects, and its lightness did not impede air movement.

Gothic Revival furniture was the style into the 1840s and its massiveness was particularly suited to bedrooms. Closets were not an architectural feature at this time; clothing was stored in large cabinets called armoires or wardrobes, usually with double, mirrored fronts, and space to hang or lay clothing. Men's clothing was stored flat.

Bedroom suites of bed, dresser with cheval mirror, and washstand, topped with marble or wood, were manufactured for middle-class homes in the cottage style. "Spool" beds were popular, nicknamed "Jenny Lind beds" because the Swedish Nightingale was rumored to have slept in one when she toured the United States.

Made of less costly woods like maple or pine, the simple furniture could be elaborately painted with floral or foliage patterns. The well-to-do preferred the more opulent style of Rococo Revival or Renaissance

Left, above: This is the bedroom of musician Jesse Shepard, as it was in 1887. The dark wood wainscoting of redwood, and classical fleur-de-lis wallpaper design, as well as the restrained style of bed, point to a gentleman's fittings. The stained glass above the doorway is one of the artisan touches to the house.

Left, below: The bedroom of Samuel Clemen's daughter, Susy, features a spool bed, also known as a Jenny Lind bed, a type of cottage furniture, mass-produced for the country home. In the upper right hand corner of the room is an air duct, indicating that the house had forced air heat, a luxury.

Right: This 1820s bedroom shows the classic English style bed, with its canopy and drapery to keep out drafts. Though the room has a fireplace, it might not have been used at night. This room was restored in 1955 by the Historic Savannah Society in Georgia.

Left: *This richly carved bed, the only ornate thing in this otherwise simple room, was Teddy Roosevelt's; this is his bedroom at Sagamore Hill. The quilt was given to him by the Emperor of Japan.*

Right: *The half-tester bed replaced the four-poster canopied bed with its full enclosure, though no draperies are hanging from this one. This room has minimal furniture, including the screen in the corner hiding the washstand. The is the guest bedroom in President Benjamin Harrison's house, restored to its 1875 appearance.*

Revival in woods of walnut, mahogany, or rosewood with carvings and applied moldings. As with other furniture in the house, golden oak, promoted by the Arts and Crafts Movement, was popular at the end of the century. Additional pieces of furniture found in the bedroom were writing desks, chaises, or other upholstered furniture.

Bedrooms of all classes were home to the odds and ends bits of furniture removed from the "public" rooms when fashion dictated. As one writer put it in an 1897 issue of *The House Beautiful,* "The bedroom is too generally neglected. The dining room and hall, the library and the parlor have infinite pains and thought bestowed upon them. Money is spent as freely as may be and effects quite charming and attractive are eagerly sought. In the bedroom it is different; any discarded chair will serve the purpose; worn carpets and faded curtains, bare walls or pictures long outgrown, in shabby frames, are here carelessly flung together. No one sees them here, it is true—no one but the very one for who the house is presupposed to be."

By the end of the century, metal-framed bedsteads of painted iron or brass provided the fresh feeling the Victorians sought. New cotton mattresses replaced earlier ones made of horsehair, or goose feathers, or the more luxurious spring mattresses of horsehair between layers of wool.

The bedroom also incorporated a dressing room, either an adjoining room or a screened off area within the bedroom. Here resided the washstand and bowl, and possibly a tin or wooden tub that was filled by hand. The chamber pot or commode was kept under the bed or sometimes in a decorative cabinet from which the pot was removed for emptying. Even after the advent of bathrooms in the home in the 1880s, the adaptation or addition of a room to be used as a bathroom was not always easily made, so the washstand remained a mainstay of the Victorian bedroom.

In large homes, husband and wife would each have a bedroom, sometimes separated by sliding doors. While the woman's room incorporated space and furniture for use as a sitting room, the man's was a room for sleeping and dressing only and was likely to be more austere. Bedrooms for couples were at the mercy of the Victorian female's affinity for patterns and fabrics, lace and tassels. It was here that the love of and emphasis on comfort could be exploited without guilt.

But still, the same *House Beautiful* article cautioned against a luxurious bedroom, "Gorgeous stuffs, inlaid or carved furniture and works of art but serve to catch the dust and distract the mind, besides cultivating a spirit of luxury which all history shows, leads straight to degeneracy." And Charles Eastlake, on the subject, "As a rule our modern bedrooms are too *fussy* in their fitting up. People continually associate the words 'luxurious and comfortable' as if they were synonymous. To my mind they convey very different ideas. Glaring chintzes, elaborate wall-papers, French polish, and rich draperies on every side may represent considerable expense and a certain order of luxury, but assuredly not comfort."

One piece of furniture that is not used much today, but was considered elementary for a Victorian woman was the chaise or bedroom couch. *House Beautiful* advised, "A lounge of some description, covered with chintz, is very necessary in a woman's room, allowing as it does, for casual 'lying downs' throughout the day." Judith Miller in *Victorian Style* found a far more practical purpose, "The Victorian lady would never sit or lie down on a made-up bed, hence the bedroom couch situated at the end of the bed. It was known as a 'fainting couch' and a lady could collapse on it if her corset was too tight!"

Rocking chairs were used in bedrooms in North America, the only room where they properly belonged, according to some. There were also slipper chairs with low seats to accommodate tying one's shoes and light-weight chairs of papier-mâché, lacquered and decorated.

Earlier, rooms were carpeted and tended to be on the dark side. Carpeting also went out with the bed drapery and wood floors became desirable, stained and varnished or painted. Area rugs used next to the bed and in other locations could be removed for cleaning. Popular color combinations were pink and blue, and red, green, and gold. Oriental rugs, then as now, were a sign of status, and in the summer straw-matting provided a cooler look.

As in the rest of the house, wallpaper was preferred, and in the bedroom the striped look was popular, followed by floral patterns. Lighter, delicate patterns were thought to be less harmful to the brain than bold ones.

Again, Charles Eastlake, "A room intended for repose ought to contain nothing which can fatigue the eye by complexity. How many an unfortunate invalid has lain helpless on his bed, condemned to puzzle out the pattern of the hangings over his head, or to stare at a wall which he feels instinctively obliged to map out into grass-plots, gravel paths and the summer-houses, like an involuntary landscape gardener?"

Wallpaper designs by William Morris and Arthur Silver were in vogue later in the era, although as people became concerned with the healthful aspects of the bedroom environment, wallpaper was discouraged because it might shelter insects. Painted walls and stained or painted paneling were preferred.

The scientific housekeeping movement cautioned against the excesses of decoration as being unsanitary. Heavy drapery was out, and light curtains of chintz with an "insertion" or "glass" of muslin or lace to soften the glare, were in.

By the end of the century, a bright, well-ventilated room with a minimum of fabric and carpeting promoted good health and a good night's sleep.

Left, above: The original 1850s furnishings in the Chatillon-DeMenil mansion show the mix and match nature of Victorian bedroom furniture. This half-tester or half-canopy bed of Greek Revival design has the drapery tied back until bedtime. The pleated silk top, along with the busily patterned wallpaper and carpet give this room a French flair, and the bassinet is Renaissance Revival.

Left, below: This is the master bedroom in President Rutherford B. Hayes' home, built 1859–63. Three bedrooms were added during renovations in 1881. The small tête at the foot of the bed serves as a resting place for the lady of the house during the day. The rocking chair finds its home here, the only place outside of the porch thought to be appropriate for it.

Entrance Halls
and Libraries

ENTRANCE HALL

In the Victorian world, an entranceway, or hall was more than a passage from the front door to the parlor, or other rooms. The entranceway in the Victorian home was there to make an impression upon the visitor, to make a statement about one's position in society and the world.

Victorian hallways were a staging area for the visit to come. Outer wraps were removed and placed on a hall tree, wet umbrellas were placed in the umbrella stand, gloves were removed by the gentlemen and placed on a convenient table or hallstand, and women checked the state of their hair or other aspect in the hall mirror. Some hallstands incorporated pegs for hanging coats, an umbrella stand, a mirror, and a shelf for objects all in one.

If visitors were coming from a hostile environment—very hot or very cold—they might be offered a comforting beverage in the hall area where there was always a settee or several chairs. If the lady or gentleman of the house were not home, the visitor would leave a calling card on a silver (or electroplated silver!) tray on the hall table. A corner of the card was folded to convey a specific meaning: right upper corner—*a visit*; right lower corner—*to take leave*; left upper corner—*congratulations*; left lower corner—*condolences*.

The entranceway often provided extra space for entertaining and, if the parlor was carpeted, could be used for dancing as the floors were generally wood with area rugs. After the 1840s, encaustic tiles made of powdered clay were set in a variety of visually stunning geometric designs, today a hallmark of a house from this era. Grandfather clocks, a mainstay of the entranceway in the early part of the century, were replaced with an astounding variety of shelf clocks as America came to dominate the clockmaking profession.

Staircases that made a sweeping or formal entrance into the hallway were highly desirable. Formerly narrowed, cramped affairs hidden behind doors, staircases grew with the home sizes into dramatic displays of interior architecture with highly carved newel posts and banisters that were works of art. Landings had seating arrangements and stained-glass windows.

Staircase building required a special knowledge and ability in geometry and structure, as well as carpentry skills. Staircase designs and pieces could be ordered by mail just like other architectural elements that were added to Victorian homes.

Left: The entrance hall of the Morris-Butler House, a Second Empire Italianate villa in Indianapolis, Indiana, sets the stage for the house's collection of Victoriana. The patterned carpet, instead of encaustic tile or wood flooring, is a luxurious touch and the hallstand serves in lieu of a closet, for outer garments.

<hr />

Above: The oak staircase descending to the entranceway of the 1892 Heritage House makes a statement of restrained elegance. Beautiful detailing and craftsmanship are evident in every aspect of the furnishings including the leaded glass window, amd tiled fireplace.

Right, above: This unusual flying staircase in the Garth Woodside mansion in Hannibal, Missouri, rises three stories. An attractive and inviting entrance hall was important to the Victorian notion of putting a good foot forward, and indicated one's higher social standing in Victorian society.

Right, below: It's difficult to imagine many visitors in this hallway at the 1868 Villa Louis, as it is so crowded with furniture. A stained-glass window adorns the landing that also has a settee. Note the statuary ready to receive calling cards in the left foreground.

Above: This graceful, two-story Montmorenci staircase at Winterthur, home of Henry Francis DuPont, was modeled after one from an 1820s house in North Carolina. The delicate lines of the Chippendale furniture complement its sweeping lines.

Left, above: This staircase in Château-sur-Mer was remodeled in 1871 by Richard Morris Hunt and is considered by scholars to be his best work. The underside is painted to resemble trailing plants on an arbor. The stained-glass window on the landing is by William McPherson of Boston.

Left, below: Entryways could be as sizeable as a room, for example 18 x 10 feet. This 1897 Queen Anne, called Copshalolm, was designed by Charles A. Rich who also designed Theodore Roosevelt's house Sagamore Hill. The staircase balcony has intricate carving reminiscent of a church.

THE LIBRARY

Books, and the reading of them, were raised to new heights in Victorian culture and in the home in particular. The Bible, above all, was a prominent book in many Victorian homes. Works on travel and self-improvement were popular, along with novels by Washington Irving, Henry James, and Charles Dickens. People actually read essays, most notably those of Ralph Waldo Emerson and Henry David Thoreau.

Books were expensive until machine-made paper made them affordable to middle-class readers. Not all houses had the luxury of devoting a separate room for a library, so books were displayed in bookcases in the parlor. But an effort was made to create a home library, partly as a symbol of a family's intellectual curiosity.

Libraries had always existed in the homes of the wealthy and traditionally tended to be the domain of the man of the house, as reflected by the décor. Wood paneling, dark colored wallpaper or other wall treatment advertised the serious purpose of the room. Built-in bookcases, or freestanding ones, some with glass doors, a desk, and comfortable furniture for reading were basic elements of the library or study. It was also a place where the gentlemen retired to after dinner for their treasured smoke and nightcap.

Edith Wharton's idea of how a library should be decorated was expressed thus, "The general decoration of the library should be of such character as to form a background or setting to the books, rather than to distract attention from them...When there are books enough, it is best to use them as part of the decorative treatment of the walls, paneling any intervening spaces in a severe and dignified style..." And, "It does not follow that because books are the chief feature of the library, other ornaments should be excluded; but they should be used with discrimination...Nowhere is the modern litter of knick-knacks and photographs more inappropriate than in the library."

Over the Victorian era, lighting ranged from fireplaces, candlelight, oil or kerosene lamps, to gas and electric lighting. In rural areas, a central hanging kerosene fixture was called a library lamp while urban homes were likely to have brass gasoliers. Light provided by electricity was cleaner and more even than gas or kerosene light, but didn't enter most middle-class homes until the end of the century. There were concerns about its safety and it was even claimed by one architect to cause freckles.

Left: The Victorian era saw a revival of the art of stained glassmaking, most notably by John La Farge and Louis Comfort Tiffany. The interest in medieval styles of architecture helped bring this art form into the home.

Right, above: The library in Samuel Clemen's (popularly known as Mark Twain) home really shows the Victorian ability to meld seemingly disparate room components into an overall harmonious effect. The built-in bookcases, fashionable colors of red and green, objects d'art of Chinese and classical origins, and the conservatory make this textbook Victorian.

Right, below: Parquet floors, brass chandeliers, oak and walnut woodwork, and few decorative items are appropriate for the Governor's study in the Park-McCullough House.

The Victorian Bathroom

So taken are we with the wonders of Victorian architecture, and the intricacies of interior accessories and furniture, that we forget what is arguably the most important contribution made by the Victorians: the bathroom.

It wasn't until the last quarter of the century that houses were built incorporating a room especially outfitted as a bathroom, although by the 1860s most homes had retrofitted bathrooms. What delayed the development of the concept of a bathroom was the installation of municipal water and waste systems, along with a workable venting system for toilets.

Interestingly enough, hotels, such as Boston's Tremont in 1829, and New York's Astor House in 1834, had indoor plumbing long before private homes. Imagine sanitary conditions before the advent of the indoor bathroom. Chamber pots (also known as *chaise percee* or commodes) were used indoors but emptying and cleaning them was an onerous task, helped by having servants. Outside, privies or outhouses were used in conjunction with the chamber pot. It's not difficult to imagine how disagreeable they were in the winter or in crowded cities.

Water closets used a discharge of water to send waste down a drain and into a sewer or cesspool. Earth closets utilized a discharge of soil to cover waste, instead of water to wash it away. In the cities, workers called dustmen were employed to remove the soil-covered waste from the privies. In 1853, Fowler, of the octagonal house, advocated water closets located under the stairs, the contents passing into a box in the cellar. Air currents from the chimney would sweep odors away.

Bathing was not quite as problematic before indoor plumbing, though it certainly was not the convenience we know. Washstands and washbowls were part of every bedroom furnishing. Bathing the entire body was done either standing in a shallow pan and sponging oneself down, or by partially immersing oneself in a hip bath. These rather elegant looking tubs with high sloping backs only accommodated part of the body, the legs hung out!

Pumping and heating the water, filling and emptying the baths, were arduous tasks, especially if the tub was in an upstairs room. Made of tin, copper, or cast iron sometimes painted to resemble marble, the tubs would be placed in front of a fireplace or stove for maximum comfort. In all but the southern and warmer western areas, bathing was certainly a hurried affair due to largely unheated rooms.

One invention created to circumvent heating the water, before emptying it into the bath, was a tub with a gas powered heater underneath that applied a flame directly to its (and the bather's!) bottom.

Left: The ceramic tile and freestanding fixtures in the Haas-Lilienthal House bathroom make it very contemporary for 1886. Only the rich would have a fully installed bathroom like this one before the 1890s.

Showers did exist. The most common were similar to the contraption that campers use today: a tank filled with water hung high, the water released by pulling a cord. A tent-like affair covered the bather. Another system had the bather hand-pump cold water up tubes that supported a tank overhead, then release it by the pull of a chain.

In the countryside, water that was hand-carried into the house was obtained from cisterns or rain barrels, or by pumps from wells. In the city, tank wagons delivered water, or it was obtained from cisterns on the house roof or in the attic. Large cities had some kind of water supply for at least some of the neighborhoods by the end of the 1870s.

Concern about hygiene and the spread of disease caused by poor sanitary conditions was more of an incentive to build functioning sewer and water systems than a desire for creature comforts. A yellow fever epidemic in Philadelphia, at the end of the eighteenth century, led to a realization of the connection between polluted drinking water and diseases. Philadelphia developed the first municipal water main with cast-iron pipes in 1804. Earlier systems used pipes of bored-out logs. Sixty-five years later, the Chicago Water Tower set an example of pumping water from Lake Michigan to supply water mains.

As sanitary sewer systems were being constructed in large municipalities, paving the way for indoor plumbing and water closets, ventilation of sewer gas was still a problem. In 1874, a breakthrough was made in venting, solving the problem of sewer gases backing up inside the house.

The toilet design that is the closest relative, mechanically speaking, to the ceramic fixture we know today, was conceived by an Englishman, Alexander Cummings, in 1775 who added a water trap under the bowl—sort of an automated chamber pot. A trial and error method to develop a workable trap for properly removing wastes and gases from the house, along with improvements in the manufacture of cast-iron and terra-cotta pipes, preceded the successful toilet. Several types of toilets were in use, but it was the so-called washout toilet, operated by a rush of water from an overhead cistern, that became the most popular.

Some toilets were incredibly beautiful in the Victorian era, if not painted like porcelain china, then at least embossed with scrolls or sea figures and other designs. That was because the manufacturers of these early toilets were companies such as British Royal Doulton, makers of fine china, and English teapot-maker Twyford.

Once the technicalities were worked out, the Victorians had their prudishness to contend with. Some toilets were disguised by having a mahogany bench with paneled front built over them. There's even an account of an upholstered velvet chair (the derivation of the nickname "throne"?) encasing a toilet in a mansion.

When the outhouse was brought indoors, it was segregated for a while, in a closet or small room, adjacent to the bathroom, then, once moved into the bathroom, set in an alcove protected by a screen or hung with *portieres*.

Before the craze for scientific housekeeping took over at the end of the century, the bathroom was like any other room in the Victorian household, in terms of wall and window treatments. Walls could be partially paneled with wooden wainscoting, then painted or wallpapered, with everything protected from condensation by coats of varnish. Floors were wooden, covered with Oriental or kilim rugs. Windows might be of stained glass for privacy and hung with the same elaborate drapery as the bedroom or parlor.

The unique feature of the first Victorian bathrooms is that tubs and sinks were enclosed in wooden surrounds to look like furniture. Pieces of additional furniture such as small tables, a shaving stand, and a chair or two contributed to the cozy atmosphere. Gas lights on either side of a wall mirror and pictures on the walls added to the effect.

At the end of the century, as the concern for hygiene increased, exposed plumbing was preferred over enclosed; the latter supposedly created a haven for germs, vermin, and mildew. The cozy warmth of the wood-lined bathroom, with its draperies and rugs, gave way to the clinical-like appearance of tile walls and freestanding porcelain fixtures, though fixtures like the claw-footed tubs and graceful pedestal sinks retained their decorative features. Because tile was costly, middle-class homes might have linoleum patterned to resemble marble on the floor and walls of painted Lincrusta or Anaglypta wallpaper.

꧁꧂

Above: *Bathroom fixtures, as we know them, were not introduced into the Victorian home until public water and sewer systems were developed, near the end of the nineteenth century. This photograph exemplifies how early bathrooms were decorated like other rooms in the home, with lavish wall and window treatments.*

꧁꧂

Above: Every modern convenience was supposedly available in this kitchen in General Grant's home in Galena, Illinois. Between the windows is a dry sink and next to it the wood box. Most stoves could burn either wood or coal.

The Victorian Kitchen

Unlike the bathroom, there was always a kitchen in the home. At first, it was an open hearth until the beginning of the nineteenth century, when the cast-iron wood or coal burning stove was introduced. That apparatus stayed around for 100 years.

Once houses were designed without an all-purpose kitchen-dining room-parlor, the kitchen, where possible, was relegated to basements or half-basements, in the British manner. In large cities, tall and narrow row houses had on their ground floor or basement (actually only a few steps below street level), a family living and dining quarter near the street entrance, and a kitchen in the back. The parlor and dining room for company were on the floor above, with the bedrooms on a third floor, creating as one wit put it, private, public, and productive areas. By the 1840s, kitchens in middle-class homes had moved above ground.

Kitchens had odors, were unbearably hot in the summer, and most of all, were a private part of family life to be shielded from public view. They were working rooms. Actually, kitchens in middle-to-upper class homes were a series of rooms, a distinction of the Victorian period.

The scullery was for washing dishes and preparing vegetables. It had a large sink of zinc, stone, or porcelain-enameled cast iron, with a wooden drainboard. If there wasn't a separate laundry room, linens were washed, ironed, and stored here in a linen press. For this, an open hearth large enough to accommodate a sizable copper or cast-iron pot was required, or a second stove to heat the water and the irons. It was estimated that 50 gallons, or 400 pounds, of water was needed to wash one batch of clothes, which included boiling, scrubbing, then rinsing, bluing, and starching them.

The kitchen itself had a large table, commonly of pine or other inexpensive wood, for food preparation and for the servant's meals, and the stove or range. Marble-topped tables were used for pastry making, and dressers or shelves provided storage for dishes and serving pieces. A pie safe, a cabinet with a screened opening in the door to circulate air, yet block flies, was also common.

For food storage, a larder with cool, slate floor or a cold or root cellar kept meats and fresh foods for a short time. By the 1860s, the icebox, at this time an insulated wooden cabinet was introduced, though it wasn't until the 1880s that it was prevalent.

The pantry (or butler's pantry in wealthier homes) was where the silver and glass-ware were stored, along with table linens. A dumb waiter, a small pulley-operated elevator, carried food up to the dining area, when the kitchen was still on a lower level. A servant's call box was also located in the pantry.

Activities that took place in these rooms included scouring pots, keeping the stove going (especially if it was connected to a hot water storage tank), caring for the stove—which included cleaning soot from flues, blacking the cast iron to keep it from rusting, and polishing its nickel-plated decoration—heating water for bathing, scrubbing floors and laundry, and ironing, which also required a stove or other source of heat (like hot coals) for the irons. Cleaning and polishing the silver, copper, and brass were also ongoing jobs.

Because servants were plentiful and affordable until the machine shops of the Industrial Revolution lured them away with higher wages, technological improvements in this area were few and far between. Once the lady of the house was forced into the kitchen, change came about rapidly.

In the 1860s and 1870s, when water supply systems began to be developed and gas became available, plumbing replaced the force pump in the kitchen sink, and boilers were introduced for heating water. At this time, cleaning products were marketed to make cleaning and caring for the kitchen easier.

The gas stove was introduced to the public in 1851, at the Crystal Palace Exhibition in London, but because it was considered dangerous and costly, it was not in common use until the end of the century. The Beecher sisters, Catharine and Harriet, in their book on domestic science, *The American Woman's Home*, advocated the coal burning stove, "With proper management of dampers, one ordinary-sized coal hod of anthracite coal will, for twenty-four hours keep the stove running, keep seventeen gallons of water hot at all hours, bake pies and puddings in the warm closet, heat flat irons under the back cover, boil tea kettle and one pot under the front cover, bake bread in the oven and cook a turkey in the tin roaster in front."

The only plausible materials for flooring in the kitchen were brick tile, or hardwood. Linoleum, a mixture of ground cork, ground wood, and linseed oil invented in the 1860s by Englishman Frederick Walton, was an instant hit for use in service areas of homes of the well-to-do. Walls were most often painted in oil enamel-based paint in colors of cream, gray, or tan with a somber wainscoting of dark green or brown. A plate rail near the ceiling was a practical decorative element.

Almon Varney's list of items necessary in a typical kitchen 1885

Wooden ware: kitchen table, wash bench, wash tubs (three sizes), wash boards, bosom board, bread board, towel roller, potato masher, wooden spoons, flour sieve, chopping bowl, soap bowl, pails, lemon squeezer, clothes wringer, clothes horse, clothes pins, clothes basket, mop, broom and wood box. *Tin ware*: boiler for clothes, boiler for ham, bread pan, two dish pans, preserving pan, four milk pans, two quart basins, two pint basins, two quart covered tin pails, one four-quart covered tin pail, sauce pans with covers (two sizes) two tin cups with handles, two pint molds (for rice, blanc-mange, etc.) one skimmer, two dippers (different sizes), one quart measure, pint and a half measures, bread pans, two round jelly cake pans, two long pie pans, coffee pot, tea steeper, steamer, horse radish grater, nutmeg grater, egg beater, cake turner, cake cutter, apple corer, potato cutter, flour dredge, tea canister, coffee canister, cake, bread, cracker and cheese boxes, crumb tray and dust pans. *Iron ware*: range or stove, pot with steamer to fit, soup kettle, preserving kettle (porcelain), tea kettle, large and small frying pans, gem pans, iron spoons of various sizes, gridiron, griddle, waffle iron, toasting rack, meat fork, can opener, coffee mill, flat irons, hammer, tack hammer, screw driver and ice pick. *Stone ware*: crocks (various sizes), bowls of pint, two quart, four quart and six quart, six earthen baking dishes of various sizes.

Left, above: This house predates the Victorian period but is a good example of pre-dining room days when the kitchen was the center of family activity. The opening on the right side of the hearth is a beehive oven for baking. Ladder-back chairs with woven-rush seats and the plainest of wooden tables complete the scene in the Millard Fillmore House.

Left, below: This is the kitchen of Abraham Lincoln, in Springfield, Illinois, where he lived during his early years as a lawyer. The kitchen stove burned all year long, as the kitchen was used for all cooking and water heating purposes.

Victorian Porches
and Gardens

The Victorians excelled in their expression of love for nature. They brought it inside when possible with houseplants and other natural objects. Wealthier homes had conservatories for indoor gardens. Exotic plants like ferns, palms, caladiums, and yucca were used, indoors and out. Likewise, they brought the indoor outside. During this epoch, garden furniture had its heyday, as gardens, and later porches, became outdoor parlors.

What brought the Victorians outside were their gardens, formally designed for the rich, less structured cottage gardens for the middle class. Lawns became part of the suburban landscape after the 1870s, and croquet was in vogue, having been introduced by the British after the Civil War. Strolls through garden paths led to cast-iron garden furniture in inviting spots.

After the 1860s, seed houses began producing and distributing seed packets by mail, giving practically anyone the opportunity to purchase a wide variety of seeds for growing flowers and vegetables. The late nineteenth century interest in health and hygiene contributed to the interest in gardening, as it was an activity that exposed the gardener to plenty of fresh air and exercise.

Like most things during the Victorian period, cultivating a garden was not without its moral purpose. According to *American Women's Home*, "In pursuing this amusement children can also be led to acquire many useful habits. Early rising would, in many cases, be thus secured; and if they were required to keep their walks and borders from weeds and rubbish, habits of order and neatness would be induced. Benevolent and social feelings could also be cultivated, by influencing children to share fruits and flowers with friends and neighbors, as well as to distribute roots and seeds to those who have not the means of procuring them."

Gardening became a mania. Commercially-made fertilizers were available in the last quarter century and horticultural societies blossomed. Of course, the Victorian penchant for decoration and control of their environment extended to the garden. Carpet bedding, flowers planted in beds shaped like crescents, stars, or other patterns, and *parterres*, flowers planted to make geometric designs, the beds sometimes sloping to better present the image, were the rage in parks, in front of municipal buildings, and in estate-sized homes.

Left: Here's a good example of the elaborate and fanciful way Victorians decorated their porches, another "public face" to the world. This view of the Morey mansion in Redlands, California, gives us only a glimpse of the eclectic nature of this Queen Anne house.

By the end of the Victorian period, the herbaceous border from England's Gertrude Jekyll replaced the formalism of carpet bedding with the casualness of wild flowers and perennials, that complemented the Arts and Crafts Movement's plea for simplicity.

Garden ornamentation included various wrought-iron stands for flowerpots, such as a tripod affair known as a gypsy stand, and cast-iron or ceramic urns. Fountains were also popular, one of the biggest selling was "Out in the Rain"—two children holding an umbrella—that could be used as a lawn ornament, or fitted with plumbing for a fountain. Gazing balls on pedestals competed with classical statuary.

The porch was an extended living area for the Victorians. As the hallway provided a transition from the outside to the interior of the home, the porch was a connection from the inside to the outside. Homes in Gothic Revival, Italianate, and, of course, the Queen Anne styles, all had some form of veranda, piazza, or porch. Summertime retreats, built in the Stick and Shingle styles, featured an abundance of porches that served to help keep houses cool, and provided plenty of outdoor entertaining space for the sociable. The octagonal house design had a step-up in this regard, as it had verandas on all sides, "allowing you to choose sun or shade, breeze or shelter from it, as comfort dictates." The parlor was moved outside as meals, teatime, and visiting took place on the porch.

Wicker furniture, with its overtones of the Far East, appealed to the late Victorians love of natural objects and plants. A wicker chair was displayed at the 1851 Crystal Palace Exhibition and sparked a wave of interest. Wicker could mean rattan, reed, or cane furniture and, at first, was as ornate as indoor parlor furniture because, in the beginning, it was used indoors. As inside furniture it was painted, usually white, but sometimes other colors, or gilded. Being lightweight, inexpensive, and cool because of its open construction, it was the perfect furniture to move outside.

Rustic and twig style furniture, originally made for mountain and lakeside homes of the rich in New York State, became fashionable. This furniture was made for the garden before it was brought onto the porch, the Adirondack chair being the most well-known of this genre. Chairs and settees made from willow were fashioned into a bentwood design. Hammocks could be simple canvas affairs or fringed with side draperies to resemble parlor furniture. Suites, such as rocker, settee, and chair, in a variety of materials were sold just like suites of parlor furniture. Cast-iron furniture was not as affordable for the middle class, one piece costing as much as a suite of parlor furniture.

Left: *The back porch of this 12 room farmhouse in 1886, gives us a behind-the-scenes look at Victorian daily living. Not all porches were for lounging and watching the world go by. The washboard in the tub against the wall and the hand-operated wringer remind us that there was much hard work behind the face that was presented to the public.*

Right: *This is Montezuma, the San Diego home of musician Jesse Shepard. The stained-glass windows represent the four seasons in this conservatory, that brings a little of the outside in. Note the encaustic floor tiles, wrought-iron and ceramic plant stands. Ferns and palms were typical Victorian plants.*

The porches reflected the Victorian penchant for decorating; sometimes porch ceilings were painted to look like the sky and the floor was always painted. Porch ornamentation could be complex, depending on the style of house. Lattice work, brackets, pillars, and gingerbread trim all contributed to create an architectural structure for this outdoor space.

Left: *It's likely that Samuel Clemens sat on this porch at the Garth Woodside mansion in Hannibal, Missouri, since he lived next door. The spaciousness and wicker furniture make it an inviting outdoor room.*

Above: *These gardens were designed to give the effect of an 1846 landscape at Woodrow Wilson's home in Staunton, Virginia. Very formal in nature they include two terraces, the lower one with boxwood-lined bowknot beds. When Wilson was born here in 1856 there were likely outbuildings and maybe a kitchen garden instead of anything so elaborate.*

Right: *The rose garden at Lyndhurst House, designed by Andrew Jackson Davis in 1838, is an outstanding example of Victorian landscaping. Millionaire Jay Gould lived here in 1880 and it's not difficult to imagine shirtwaisted ladies with parasols strolling under the arches.*

Bibliography

Baer, Morley; *Painted Ladies: San Francisco's Resplendent Victorians*; New York: Dutton, 1978.

Beecher, Catharine Esther; *The American Woman's Home: or Principles of Domestic Science; Being a Guide to the Formation and Maintenance of Economical, Healthful, Beautiful and Christian Homes*; New York: J.B. Ford & Co., c. 1869.

Bishop, Robert and Coblentz, Patricia; *The World of Antiques, Art, and Architecture in Victorian America*; New York: Dutton, c. 1979.

Clark, Clifford Edward, Jr; *The American Family Home, 1800-1960*; Chapel Hill: University of North Carolina Press, c. 1986.

Eastlake, Charles L.; *Hints on Household Taste in Furniture, Upholstery, and Other Details*; Boston: J.R. Osgood & Co., 1872.

Edwards, Clive D.; *Victorian Furniture: Technology & Design*; Manchester: Manchester University Press, c. 1993.

Foley, Mary Mix; *The American House*; New York: Harper & Row, c. 1980.

Foy, Jessica H. and Schlereth, Thomas J. ed; *American Home Life, 1880-1930: A Social History of Spaces and Services*; Knoxville, University of Tennessee Press, c. 1992.

Garrett, Wendell; *Victorian America: Classical Romanticism to Gilded Opulence*. New York: Rizzoli, c. 1993.

Grier, Katherine; *Culture & Comfort: Parlor Making and Middle Class Identity, 1850-1930*; Washington: Smithsonian Institution Press, 1988.

Grow, Lawrence; *American Victorian: A Style & Source Book*; New York: Harper & Row, 1984.

Howe, Barbara J. [et al.]; *Houses and Homes: Exploring Their History*; Nashville, Tenn. American Association for State and Local History, c. 1987.

Holmes, Kristin; *The Victorian Express*; Wilsonville, Or.: Beautiful America Pub. Co., c. 1991.

Livingston, Kathryn; *Victorian Interiors: Room by Room*; Gloucester, Mass.: Rockport Publishers, c1999.

McAlester, Virginia and Lee; *A Field Guide to American Houses*; New York, Knopf, c. 1984.

McAlester, Virginia; *Great American Houses and Their Architectural Styles*; New York: Abbeville Press, c. 1994.

Madigan, Mary Jean Smith; *Eastlake Influenced American Furniture, 1870-1890*; [catalog of an exhibition] November 18, 1973-January 6, 1974, the Hudson River Museum. Yonkers, N.Y.: Hudson River Museum, 1973.

Miller, Judith; *Victorian Style*; London: M. Beazley, c. 1993.

Plante, Ellen M; *The Victorian Home: The Grandeur and Comforts of the Victorian Era, in Households Past and Present*; Philadelphia, Pa.: Running Press, c. 1995.

Schlereth, Thomas J.; *Victorian America: Transformations in Everyday Life, 1876-1915*; New York: HarperCollins, c. 1991.

Stevenson, Louise L.; *The Victorian Homefront, American Thought and Culture, 1860-1880*; New York: Twayne Publishers, c. 1991.

Varney, Almon Clother; *Our Homes and Their Adornments, or, How to Build, Finish, Furnish & Adorn a Home: a Complete Household Cyclopedia Designed to Make Happy Homes for Happy People*; Detroit: J.C. Chilton, 1885.